START TO FINISH

AN AUTHOR'S HOW-TO BOXSET

WAHIDA CLARK

Wahida Clark Distribution
60 Evergreen Place
Suite 904A
East Orange, New Jersey 07018
1-866-910-6920
www.wclarkdistribution.com
www.wclarkpublishing.com

Copyright 2022 © by Wahida Clark
All rights reserved. This book, or parts thereof, may not be reproduced in any form without permission.

Library of Congress Cataloging-In-Publication Data:
Wahida Clark
Start to Finish: An Author's How-To Boxset
ISBN 978-1-954161-93-1 (eBook)
ISBN 978-1-954161-95-5 (Paperback)
ISBN 978-1-954161-94-8 (Audiobook)

1. Writing- 2. Book Publishing 3. References- 4. Book Distribution- 5. Coaching
Creative Direction by Nuance Art LLC
Layout by Caroline Zonis
Art Supplied Gfx
www.artdiggs.com
Printed in USA

HOW TO TURN YOUR MESSAGE OR EXPERTISE INTO A PROFITABLE BEST-SELLING BOOK 2.0

MY MISSION

My mission should you choose to accept, is to make sure that in 45 days or less you seize this moment. It's finally time to get that draft, outline or book you've been struggling to write into the hands of people who need it. With the weight of accomplishment off your shoulders and another big win is under your belt, you can use your book to spread your message. Now is the time to establish yourself as the expert and get ahead of the competition!

FOREWORD

By Four-Time New York Times Bestseller ... WAHIDA CLARK!

No! Your Book doesn't have to be 300 pages! This is the answer to one of the most frequent questions that I am asked.

YOU are the Expert. You are trying to get YOUR Message across. You are focused on bringing awareness to YOUR Cause.

In today's social media, it's all about "tell me what's in it for me, tell it to me fast, is what you are trying to tell me going to help solve my problem now, or at least point me in the right direction or climate" ... Long is wrong!

Get to the point. That's what this book does, and that is what this book will show you how to do.

This book is all about Turning your Message, Cause, Expertise, or your Business Card into a Book, just like this.

1
INTRODUCTION

"You may not get rich off your book, but you can get rich because of it." – Wahida Clark

The book business has been good to me. The business of books has taken me on a journey that most authors only dream of. So, I know first-hand that having a book or being an author or expert/author can give you instant celebrity status. Because of my books I've rubbed elbows with platinum selling and Grammy award-winning artists, *New York Times* bestselling authors, actors, actresses, the top comedians, NFL, NBA, and MLB players, rappers, you name it . . . Yes, this has been my networking experience all because of being an author. I get called to do speaking engagements and get flown in to host book events and parties. I am asked to be a guest on talk, TV, and podcast shows.

Having a book opens doors you had no clue that you had a key to. And like I said, "You may not get rich off your book, but you can get rich because of it." My books have made it possible for me to receive six-figure advances, and now I am in negotiations for TV and movie deals. My books provide me with a monthly income, residual. Meaning, while I am asleep my books are selling.

A book can give you power. If you don't have one yet, continue reading...

How To Turn your Expertise into a Profitable, Bestselling Book ... Like This, is obviously the title of this book. But my first choice for the title and what this book is really about is, How To Turn Your Message, Cause, Expertise, or Your Business Card into a Book Just Like This!

But welcome to the 21st Century Social-Media-Era, in which all marketing has been taken to the latest stratosphere! There are so many ways to market a book: YouTube, Facebook, Instagram, Roku, Fire TV, **Tik-Tok, Clubhouse**... the list goes on and on and on. And the fantastic thing is all of these marketing platforms include the oldest but time-tested trend where AUTHORS are considered the EXPERTS and the new money getting ROCK STARS!

True Story. I recall seeing a *TV Segment* of Stacey Abrams on the campaign trail as she was running for Governor of Georgia. I thought, *she is an excellent speaker. She's smart and comes across as very warm and genuine.* I made a mental note that I would love to get to know her and interview her. However, I still came away only partly clear on what she actually stood for or what she believed. I wanted her to really sell me. And of course, that's when it hit me! If she had a book like this, she would have the time and space needed to lay out her message or outline her agenda, mission, and beliefs, so that she could reach her base or potential base. Ms. Abrams would then ignite! Those were my personal thoughts and opinion. And yes, you probably guessed it, she now has a book published. But when I first wrote this she didn't.

Whatever your message is, be it Mental Health, Politics, The Healing Effects of Cannabis, Human Trafficking, Women's Empowerment, Climate Change, Branding, Children and Video Games, Pool

Maintenance, you name it . . . They all can be easily put into a book just like this.

But not only will a book like this get your message across in great detail, it is simple to put together and it sets you up for future paid speaking engagements, your very own talk or TV show, more clients, and so much more.

If you were at a conference or event amongst your colleagues or peers, and the panelist introduced everyone, and you were the only one who had "author" added to your profile, who do you think the audience would gravitate toward? Who do you think the attendees would rather do business with?

Being an author gives you an edge over your competition, peers, and colleagues; authorship further propels you as the more knowledgeable expert in the eyes of your prospects.

A book just like this is the best business card you can have, the best salesman you can have, and by far the best spokesman you could have. Why? Nothing beats attending a conference or an event where everyone is handing out regular business cards, and you are handing out copies of your signed book with your regular business card tucked inside.

Remember:

An author is considered the expert. Customers and clients prefer to buy from experts over the non-expert or amateur. Your base prospects (audience) will understand or get your full message or cause if everything is laid out in a book. Below is a list of reasons your message in book format will reach your intended target:

Experts have experience.
Experts have credibility.
Experts have solutions.
Experts have authority.
Experts are leaders.

Experts have celebrity.
Experts create opportunity.
Experts can get you where you want to be.

REST ASSURED your message will not be glossed over. What you stand for will be in black and white. What you are advocating for and why will be clearly spelled out.

Becoming an Author

Anyone can become an author as long as they have something to say that people would like to read, learn, or become aware of. Becoming an author doesn't have to be difficult. And why this is great for you is, I am a four-time *New York Times* Best Seller. My team and I can assist you every step of the way! With the help of my expert publishing and branding team, you will be well on your way to becoming an author in no time. And for you authors and experts who are ready to take it to the next level, with the help of my marketing and branding team, you can launch or relaunch your book like a Rock Star!

Don't forget this book is really about, **"How to Turn Your Message, Cause, Expertise, or Your Business Card into a Book** Just Like this!" And the best part is, it doesn't have to be perfect the 1st time around. This book is version 2.0.

And yes, a business card turned into a book makes you an author, but it also establishes you as an expert. The act of you championing your cause or sharing your message and expertise on the pages of a book like this will make you an author. Your book can be on sale on Amazon, Barnes and Noble, Apple Books and on many other leading retailers.

A book like this can be the foundation of a new or existing

business that can generate multiple revenue streams. (Another Topic for Later lol)

Why You Need a Book

Everyone who has something to share or teach that can benefit others needs to write a book. Be it a message, cause, or you simply sharing your expertise. Writing a book can be easy to do, and you can write anything that your heart desires that people will be interested in reading. A 30 - 90-page book like this one is the ultimate sales tool, business card, and platform to get your message out.

Traditional business cards are always thrown away and forgotten, so you need to take the next step, and go the extra mile in creating the ultimate business card: a book just like this.

You don't have to write a long book, as long as you have valuable information that gets your point across. Writing a book is a new way to market and promote yourself, what you know, what you have experienced in the past, and what you stand for or against. If you are a business professional, then you need to write a book. If you are a celebrity, then you need to write a book. Anyone who has something important to say or something that people would like to learn needs to write a book. At the end of the day, it's about connecting with your audience and your clients. A book is *the* personal marketing tool. It's as simple as that, and I can't stress that enough.

Reasons You Need a Book

There are many excellent reasons professionals such as doctors, lawyers, celebrities, and dentists should write a book. For those who are in the medical profession, the average consumer wants to learn about new medical breakthroughs and ways that they can live a healthier life without having to sift through scientific journals filled with medical jargon. For attorneys, people want to learn how they can win court cases and how to file bankruptcy, lawsuits, etc. Celebrities, along with successful entrepreneurs, have raving fans, and they all want to know how you worked your way up to becoming a success! There are so many reasons you should write a book, and people WILL want to read what you have to say! You can become an awesome success story once you become an awesome author of your own book!

Your Message, Your Cause, Your Expertise, or The Business Card Turned Book is Right for You and Your Profession

Let me share an example. Let's say you need braces. You visit two orthodontists in the same professional complex. The first orthodontist gives you a consultation and his business card. The other orthodontist, after the consultation, hands you a book titled *Braces vs. Dental Implants. Get the facts. Know Which Procedure is Right for You.* With all else being equal, which orthodontist would you most likely schedule an appointment with? Which "business card" would you be more likely to look at again?

Being an author in your field immediately gives you credibility and authority. Others will see you as the expert that you are and having a book will help you stand out from your competition. Since books are vehicles to deliver information, books also give you a way to provide instant value to your potential customers, establishing trust. Your client gets to know a little about you. Words are powerful on a page. The true you is on display, and the potential client will decide whether to do busines with you or not. Reminder: this book is a 24 hour mouthpiece. Your message needs to target your ideal client and let them know without out a doubt that your expertise will make their lives easier or get that want satisfied.

In this case I'm telling you how easy it is to get that book written!

By detailing your expertise (what you do and why you do it, and how it benefits the reader/prospect) in a book, you can win over prospects and turn them into customers and clients.

Below are just a few professions/businesses that would benefit from a Business Card turned into a Book:

Architects
Accountants
Acupuncturists
Acting Coaches
Addiction Therapists
Chefs
Chiropractors
Coaches
Consultants
CPAs
Dance Instructors
Dentists
Dieticians
Deejays
Dog Trainers
Electricians
Event Planners
General Contractors
Hair Stylists
Home Improvement Specialists
House Painters
Landscapers
Massage Therapists
Mechanics
Mental Health Counselors
Occupational Therapists
Orthodontists

Personal Trainers
Gyms
Physical Therapists
Physicians
Plumbers
Pool Specialists
Rappers
Realtors
Restaurants
Roofers
Speakers
Tax Preparers
Tutors
Vets
Website Designers
Wedding Planners
And the list goes on . . . and on . . . and on . . . . .

**Your Clients and Prospects are Better Educated About Your Business with
a Book Like this**

All you do is compile the basic "FAQs" (Frequently Asked Questions) and "SAQs" (Should Ask Questions) about your business, expertise, message, or cause. Answer them, put them in order of importance and group them and that will get your message across and educate your prospect. It will save you a lot of time delivering your usual introductory information, and it is your automated sales rep who never sleeps and who always nails the presentation 100% of the time. You even get to sell without being salesy! Your book becomes a vehicle to educate your prospects about your business, products and services, systems, and message about you.

You are actually magnifying recognition for your personal

brand and increasing sales without salespeople. A book allows you to have a one-on-one with many people at the same time. When a prospect or client is reading your book, they are focused on you. You will be getting your message across quickly, thoroughly, and easily.

A book is an awesome networking tool. It helps you interact with all the people you want, delivering exactly what you want to say, without taking a lot of time.

You Will Achieve Better Results from Your Advertising

Use it to promote a webinar, teleseminar, or any presentation. Having made your prospects simply AWARE that you have a book heightens that awareness.

You can talk about the book or show the book in your advertising as a credibility booster and get higher responses.

- Ads Capture Attention for seconds
- Books holds the attention much longer
- Books, even short ones, leave a mark on the reader that usually gets them talking about it to others
- Ads are impersonal; books are always attached to their author
- A book shows your commitment, which readers will find impressive

Books Have Longevity and Viral Power – Since They Are Not Thrown Away

BOOKS DON'T GET LOST in a drawer like a business card does. Books rest on shelves, desks, and countertops, in bathrooms, inside backpacks; and they are stored on e-reading devices. Books do not get tossed into the trash like sales letters or postcards. People just don't throw away books. They might get packed away. They might get donated or given away, but they are very rarely, if ever, trashed. I recall when moving, placing some books in the trash and then a few minutes later, taking them out! I just couldn't throw them away. Ever go to a flea market or auction and see a box of books? What is that natural instinct? To go through them. It is so exciting because you never know what magic or wisdom you may come across. Is there a better vehicle to deliver your message that is so widely valued and not disposed of within minutes? I don't think so.

We at W. Clark Distribution Media and Publishing Will Eliminate the Common Excuses for not Getting Your Book Completed!

Such as:

- I want to ... but I'll eventually get around to it one of these days
- I don't have time
- I don't know how
- I'm not a writer
- I don't know what to write about

If you are still thinking there is no way you can write a book, remember that it doesn't have to be long. Simply brainstorm topics by thinking of questions you are asked most frequently. From that list you can create a book. And you don't have to give away all of your knowledge in one book. Just give away one very specific nugget, filled with value that your potential clients would appreciate and thank you for.

Is Writing a Book for You?: The Answer to that is Yes, if:

- *you* want to speak at events or be interviewed on podcasts or talk shows
- *you* consider your business to be "missional"
- there are frequently asked questions that you have to answer for each new client
- *you* want to record lessons you learned
- *you* want to communicate principles you wish to pass on to others
- *you* have content that you can repurpose (republish) (blogs, articles, interviews, e-books, reports, etc.)
- *you* are running for any kind of public office
- *and more...*

Leveraging Your Book

Having your expertise, message, cause, or business card turned into a book gets even better! It can be used as leverage for greater opportunities. For some it might be speaking engagements, for others it might be product sales, and for you it might be getting more clients. If you are running for Governor, Senator, or President, it can be used as a fundraising tool and getting your message across to your potential base.

A book becomes another resource in your marketing funnel to lead them to your back-end offer. This means that you need to offer your readers, on top of great content and readability, a clear and direct call to action within your book. Even if they don't ever read a word, it needs to be clear to the person who is aware of your book what they need to do next and how to do business with you. But more important, *how you can serve.*

How your book can generate sales without being a Best Seller

Give it Away on Your Website as a Lead-generating Offer.

Sounds absurd right? It's not. Remember: Your book is your 24-7, 365 days a year salesperson. Offering your book as a giveaway, now positions a potential prospect to enter in to your sales funnel. In exchange for the FREE book you can collect names, e-mail addresses, and phone numbers, then move them directly to your follow-up campaign or onto an order page. Be sure to have your website/funnel, or any reference to a free report, webinar, etc., sprinkled throughout your booklet.

Depending on your offer, you can even ask for a small amount of money, e.g. $6.99 for processing and shipping and oftentimes gain *a better and more qualified* prospect. That is something that you would have to measure.

2
OTHER WAYS TO BUILD A BUSINESS WITH A BOOK

A Book Just like This can be used to get you high paid speaking gigs.

Who loves public speakers?

- Non-profit groups
- Meeting Planners
- Religious Organizations
- Government and State Institutions
- Talk Show and Television Hosts
- And many, many more!

Create a Buzz in Your Industry so People Will Take Notice of You

If you want people in your industry to recognize your name, then you need to write, publish, and promote your book! Books get handed around, borrowed, loaned, talked about all the time. People know about/ rave about authors they have never read, which shows how just the act of writing a book gives off a great impression.

Send an Industry-Wide Message When You Write a Book

Do you consider yourself to be a Subject Matter Expert (SME) or guru in the industry you work in? Are you a doctor, lawyer, marketer, or other professional that has something to say to everyone who works in the same industry?

People are always seeking out more knowledge so they can improve their:

- Lives
- Health
- Careers
- Family
- Finances

If people believe you have something valuable in your book, they're going to buy your book and read it! They're also going to spread the word to as many people as they know!

Become a Subject Matter Expert (SME) In Your Profession!

To become a widely known SME, or to communicate to a large number of people, you need to become an author. This is the only way people will listen to what you have to say and believe that you are an SME in your profession or industry. Do you have knowledge about the:

- Health and Medical Industry?
- Fashion Industry?
- Legal Industry?
- Retail Industry?

- Celebrity Living?
- Cannabis Industry?
- Bitcoin Industry?
- Or Anything Else from the Endless List of Topics to Choose from?

If you are a wealth of information in any industry or profession, then you need to write a book! That is one of the *only ways* you will be able to share secrets, tips, and advice effectively, with millions of people worldwide!

In my opinion, books are valuable because they're (mostly) accessible for everyone. Entry level or seasoned profession, rich or poor, if you can read you can pick up a book and learn something. However, it is also exclusive because the act of reading is almost like hearing a secret. It's personal between author and reader. That is what makes books so impactful; it's a very personal thing to read a book.

Use A Book Just Like This as an Additional Revenue Stream

A book can become an income stream. Thousands of companies buy books in bulk every year to use as premiums, gifts, employee training, marketing tools, etc. So, keep that in mind when putting your book together and do so accordingly.

Remember: What this book is really about is, "How To Turn your Message, Cause, Expertise, or your Business Card into a Book Just like this!"

The Different Types of Book That You Write

List Book

A *List Book* is an easy book to create and depending on the topic, can be extremely valuable to your audience. A *List Book* is simply that: a book that lists information. Why lists? Because they make it easy to brainstorm, organize, and write quickly and lists are easy to read. People love to read lists. And a good example of a List Book is: A general contractor creating a book that lists the repairs he specializes in, or "The 8 Ways a Leak Can Damage Your Home."

FAQ/SAQ Books (Frequently Asked Questions/Should Ask Questions)

This type of book is our most popular.

A plastic surgeon could write a *SAQ* Book on the types of questions a patient should ask before getting liposuction. A literary agent could write a FAQ Book on how to acquire a major publisher, or the roles of a literary agent. The most frequently asked questions and your should ask questions are combined to create one of the most powerful and compelling, revenue generated books you can think of. It will serve as the key to all your client's locked doors."

How-To Books

One of the biggest benefits of writing a How-To Book, in addition to it being extremely valuable, or that How-To Books are so easy to turn into courses, is that in many cases the bulk of the book can be pictures, not words.

What do you know that others don't? You'd be surprised at how many things you know that others would love to learn. Business "How-To" books are usually top sellers. Our team will show you how easily this is done.

FYI. Half the books on the New York Times Best Seller List between 2006 &2016 were non- fiction.

Turning Your Business Card Into a Book

One of my editors, Alanna, commented on this manuscript.

She said, "Wahida, I see how you can Turn Your Message, Cause, or Expertise into a Book, but your Business Card? You've gone too far!"

I thank her for that question because if she is a skeptic or just can't fathom how to do such a thing, that means there may be more of you skeptics out there!

So, let me give you an example. I went to my junk drawer and pulled out a random business card. (You know, that junk drawer where you toss all of the cards, loose change, pens, candy, etc., in.) Case in point, that's *exactly* why you need to turn your Business Card into a Book, so your card *won't* get tossed in a drawer somewhere and forgotten! You can't get new business that way.

I dug deep and pulled a random card that said:

Onyx
Dyson Dinsmore, CCIM
Senior Property Manager

Now, for us business folks, our job is to get new clients and spread the word about what we do to get more clients. It's not rocket science . . . If we have no clients, we have no business. Pure and simple. So, when I looked at this card, I asked:

1. ONYX. What does that mean?
2. What kind of business is ONYX?
3. What exactly does Mr. Dinsmore do?
4. What does CCIM stand for?
5. Senior Property Manager. What are the responsibilities of a Senior Property Manager?
6. Manage what? Hotels, Bars, Apartments, Nursing Homes—what?
7. Whatever you manage, why is that your specialty?
8. Why do I need a property manager? Especially you?

9. What makes your Property Management Company different from the one down the street?
10. How would you enhance my property?
11. How would you make my life easier/better?

I hope you get the picture. All Mr. Dinsmore has to do now is add another 10–15 questions about what he does, how he does it, why I need him, fill in the answers, and voilà! He has a book just like this one! Your 24 hour a day, 365 day a year assistant that is always on call for the client.

Also, another method I learned, you can place a Quick Response Code (QR Code) on a flyer or newsletter or actual business card that, when scanned, will lead directly to your book on Amazon, Barnes & Noble, or iBooks stores. I know it sounds boring or even difficult, but it is effective. It works.

Any book that you decide to write, we can help you with. Just shoot me an email at booking@wahidathecoach.com

Looking forward to partnering with you,

Wahida Clark,

Your #1 Cheerleader

3

GETTING STARTED

How About My Book Title? How Do I Come Up with One?

This to me is one of the most exciting parts about writing! Coming up with the title. And yet for some, one of the most stressful parts. Some authors begin writing their book already knowing their title. Sometimes the title doesn't hit you until after you've written your book. Sometimes a sentence will stand out or scream at you. And that's your title. But when the right title hits you, you'll know it because it's magical.

My first title was first suggested to me by my husband. I shot it down immediately because I didn't think it was cool enough. However, I made a list of titles that I thought would be best, stuck his suggestion in the middle and took a poll. When the results came back, his suggestion, *'Thugs and The Women Who Love Them'* was the winning title hands down. That tile launched my Best-Selling Book career and publishing company. Thanks hubby!!

Does the Book Cover Design Really Matter?

Absolutely! Your cover design can make or break your book. Some authors even test their designs. Meaning they post two to three designs and see which one gets the most views or positive comments. Yes, it is that serious. So, word of caution: do not cut corners when it comes to your cover or interior design. Remember: You get what you pay for. If you pay $35 for a book cover, it most likely is going to look like a $35 book cover. A basic cover design *starts* around $250 and up. However, a very good graphic designer for a cover grosses anywhere from $350 - $1,000. It all depends on how intricate, professional, and glamorous you want your cover to be.

You don't want to take a chance at choosing a book cover design that doesn't attract anyone that you're targeting. By testing out a few covers, you will soon find which one draws the most readers and traffic to your site to buy your book. And you want your book to look both fabulous and professional. You don't want to send Oprah a book that looks as if your cover and or interior (a double no-no) was designed right there on your smart phone. Be sure to request or click here for my Book Cover Check List. Or click this link here for VIP book design services.

I Don't Know the First Thing about Editing or Interior Book Design. Now What?

The majority of people who write their own book don't know anything about editing or book design. There are plenty of freelance editors and graphic designers that you can choose from online. You may want to first start out by looking into referrals or recommendations before you hire a freelancer from one of the freelance websites. You can also find good editors and designers on sites such as Freelancer, Fiverr, LinkedIn and Upwork. But again *remember*, you get what you pay for. If you pay someone pennies on the dollar, then chances are, your graphic designer or editor will not produce the results you are expecting.

Editing usually starts at around $2 - $4 per page and some start even higher. Interior Book Design can start around $75-$150 depending on the pages of the book.

So, you need to do your research before you hire someone that you don't know online, especially if you have a limited budget! Be diligent, get references, and look at samples before hiring an online freelancer to perform your editing or interior layout for your book. And here's a TIP: Your book is a reflection of you. Don't hold back when it comes to adding your personality. The best team will prioritize your voice and message.

Why Do I Need a Website or Funnel to Promote My Book?

Technology is always evolving and changing, so you will need to stay on top of the new ways to promote your book. The Internet and Social Media are at the top of the list when it comes to the best ways to promote your book and placing it in front of millions of people who are interested in the topic you are writing about. But the word around the industry, is that websites are dead funnels are the replacement. For now, I use both. We have a website for each of our businesses, however, we have almost a hundred funnels. With a software called Clickfunnels, you can sell thousands of book if you have the right funnel and the right book. Click Here to sign up for Clickfunnels via my affiliate link: (please note that I am one of their affiliates, and I do get compensation).

This is the Internet and Social Media age. If Mrs. Marbles the Cat has a website, shouldn't you have one to promote your business, yourself, or your product? A book and a website go hand in hand. Your website is also your store to sell your books, services, and products. You will want to find a web designer that has experience in creating websites for authors so you can get the best chance at selling your book online.

Trying to find the perfect web designer or funnel builder, especially if you are not technical to me, is challenging. It will take time and research, but you have to commit and get it done. Your website and funnels are just like your book: 24 hour sales person. It is your foundation to your business, you have to make sure it is strong and sound. If you don't do it. Hire someone that will get it done.

However, if you only want to sell minimal copies of your book without a website, you can simply use Amazon, Apple Books, and Barnes and Noble in hopes that they will send the traffic to your book.

Pass your Message, Cause, Expertise, or Business Card turned into a Book to:

- editors of newspapers, blogs, and magazines to get interviews or a request to write articles
- book reviewers
- radio shows and podcast hosts for interviews
- promoters that host events and get speaking gigs
- clients as gifts
- list owners to get a teleseminar or webinar gig
- librarians and institutions
- associations and trade group leaders
- sell your coaching/consulting
- powerful or famous people you want to meet
- prospects who respond to an advertisement

Pass your book out at:

- places where your prospects might run into it
- business conferences
- business meetings

- speaking events where you are not selling

Make it available as:

- a bonus with a product or with your services
- a Kindle Book to get viral traction
- a free book offer on Social Media to your targeted prospects
- a requirement for new clients to read
- a reward for sticking around for a presentation
- a thank you gift to clients
- a promo tool when you do interviews for all types of media

Last but not least, and my favorite *give it away* to secure appointments and generate referrals or leads

"Just by showing up, you will get a gift valued at $9.95!" Gifting your book will create client loyalty and you can double your client retention.

Also, use the book to generate quality referrals, especially since over 70% of new clients come from referrals. Give it away to clients and ask them to pass it along to their family, friends, and colleagues. The book will guarantee that your message is delivered exactly the way you want it.

What if I want to Write Fiction, a Memoir, My Life Story, or a Children's Book?

That's not a problem. Again, I am a 4-time *New York Times* Best-Selling Author, with a winning team of experts, editors, writers, branding coaches, marketers and more. So, connecting you with the Write (pun intended) team who wants to see you win is a bonus. If you win, we win! That is the easy part.

Writing a fictional book is not easy. I don't care what anyone else says. Personally, I've written 22 or more books that are published and in print . . . writing a book is hard work and it takes discipline. I remember writing on deadline, and we had our first beautiful, spring day in New Jersey. The springtime breeze was blowing through my window. I heard children playing and laughing, car horns honking, and music thumping through the car speakers. This was in 2008. But I was stuck inside writing while everyone else was out there enjoying the beginning of spring. Or you could be on a writing deadline while the entire family is headed out to the movies. You could be on deadline and it's 1:30 in the morning. While everyone is in a deep comatose sleep, you wish you were too, but instead you are up writing. That can be hard. Writing fiction, memoirs, and biographies is HARD WORK. However, it is can be one of the most fulfilling and self- healing endeavors you accomplish.

But . . . I Don't Know What to Write or How to Even Get Started. What Do I Do?

That's simple, and this is where we come in. If you are an entrepreneur or a celebrity, you first have to decide if you are going to do a List Book, How-To, or a FAQ/SAQ Book. If you are writing your List Book, start making your list. If you are writing the FAQ/SAQ Book, then you should jot down at least 10 questions that you are asked the most and 10 questions that you want your potential clients to ask. Then we will take it from there. Doing that simple task will allow our professional editorial staff to develop your book with you. If you want to write a tell-all, memoir, fiction, or TV script, email us at editor@wclarkdistribution.com. One of our editors will make sure you get details about our other coaching programs.

It's Easy to Get Started!

Now that you are ready to write a book, it's easy to get started! All you need to do is contact us at W. Clark Distribution, Media and Publishing Company and we'll walk you through the process. We guarantee it'll be painless, and you will be able to make your own decisions on what you want your book to have in it. We will help you take your business card, message, cause or expertise and turn it into an amazing book/booklet that you can use as a lead generator or promotional tool. You don't have any reason to not write a book!

The following is an example of what you can include in your book. I've inserted my Book Writing and Coaching Programs, as well as details for my Book Distribution Programs for the author or indie publisher. I'm sure that you already have material that you can insert in your book as well. However, this information is in real time and can be used NOW! I'm knocking down all of your excuses!

4

ON BOOK DISTRIBUTION

Nothing moves without distribution. Distribution, according to *Webster's Dictionary*, means: "to divide among many; spread or hand out."

So, if you are selling a product, book, CD, wig, etc., the wider and deeper your distribution platform, the more movement you have, the more revenue you create—and the more money you make.

And focused *Book Distribution* takes your book or books and makes them available to as many readers as possible in every way possible and gives it to them in the exact format they would like to read it.

So, you've written your book, and now, you are ready to sell it! It's mind-boggling to me why you go through all of that hard work of writing a book . . . to only sell it one way. Why leave all of that money on the table?

My ideal client writes to generate residual income from their books. The *W. Clark Distribution* platform was devised with that ideal client in mind. The authors who would benefit the most from my program are:

- You have written a book/s but only offer it to readers on Kindle
- You currently don't sell or market paperback versions of your book
- You are not in bookstores
- The audiobook, hardcover, libraries, Nook, Apple Book, large print consumers are simply out of luck because your book/s is not available on those platforms.

Distribution is EVERYTHING! We as authors hustle and grind, pulling countless all-nighters to get a book finished, so why not position ourselves to reap the maximum reward? Therefore, I MUST REPEAT!!! Why sell your book only on Amazon? Why sell your book only as an e-book? Why not sell paperbacks? Why not large print? Why not hardbacks? Why not on Kobo? Why not on Nook? Why not in the libraries? Audio books? *Why limit and block your book sales?*

In the *W. Clark Distribution* closed Facebook Group, this is where authors and small publishers can come, network, learn, and build your distribution platform. Do you need me in order for you to learn how to build your distribution platform? Yes and No! Do you need to use my Distribution Company to set up distribution for your titles? Yes and No! Here is the link to sign up for distribution with the world's largest book wholesalers, *Ingram Spark Pro*, http://www.awin1.com/awclick.php?mid=4032&id=559809 (please note that I am one of their affiliates, and I do get compensation). Go Ahead! It's FREE! Click Now!

So, not everyone needs me. But I do say YES! to the authors who e-mail me and say, "Wahida, I understand that publishing is a business, and books are not written to be sold on just one platform. I also understand that in order to sell books, I have to invest in the marketing and distribution (meaning time and money) of my book/s. I don't have the time to figure this all out for myself." Me and my Team are now available to work with you as your personal publishing and book writing coach.

I am also saying YES! to those authors who constantly e-mail me and ask how to launch, re-launch and distribute their book/s. This is YOUR opportunity to work with me. This program is for YOU, the author who wants to work with a 4x (Four-Time New York Times Best-Selling Author) NYT Best Seller of 3 Best-Selling series and Publisher of over 100 novels, including 10 Series, Celebrity Ghostwriter, and Business Book Coach.

At *W. Clark Distribution*, we take advantage and embrace current Print-on-Demand (POD) technology. We love it because it turns authors into publishers without having to warehouse inventory, take chances on projected sales, and authors don't have to invest heavily on packing supplies and shipping of boxes and endless trips to the post office while they waste time standing in line.

But the key in utilizing the POD technology is you must have the right wholesale partners and have your book pricing right, cover design marketable and much, much more, to get in bookstores and libraries.

Now, you don't have to go with learning all about book distribution, formatting, and price points alone. The *W. Clark Distribution Program* shows authors and small publishers **HOW TO SELL MORE BOOKS** by positioning their title in every possible format, meaning, e-book, paperback, hardback, large print, and audio by simply utilizing the *W. Clark All-Formats and Book Publishing and Marketing Checklist* . . . all while having *Wahida Clark*, a four-time NYT Best-Selling Author and Award Winning Independent Publisher, as YOUR personal coach! It doesn't get any better than that! Go at it alone . . . or Team Up with Wahida!

If you make the investment in time and consistency (do the

work), then in 90 days, your title will be in every format, and you are at least 3X'ing (tripling) your book sales. And you get to work with a four-time New York Times Best-Selling Author and Team up with an official and established book brand and platform. You won't find a better accountability team!

YOU CAN START BY DOWNLOADING AND USING OUR CHECKLISTS! WHEN IMPLEMENTED, THEY ARE EFFECTIVE! THEY GET YOU RESULTS!

Let's make it happen!So, there you have it! I've shared with you, how to write, what to write, and priceless info on design and book distribution. All you have to do now is apply it. For those of you who feel that you may need a little more hand holding or one-on-one support here are our packages:

Coaching Programs Available

"Twenty Minute "What to do Next" Coaching Program

This program is for you if:

1. You are working on your book project and feeling STUCK
2. You are procrastinating or worrying about the structure of your book, what to do next or finding the right audience to target
3. You have been anxiously hoping to work with four-time *New York Times* Best Seller and Publisher, Wahida Clark to give you guidance on your Book Project

What you Get: a twenty (20) minute One-on-One Strategy and Coaching Call. All is required of you is to show up on the Coaching Call with your questions, comments, or ideas ready! Not only will Wahida provide you with solutions to getting your book written, she will also put you on the road to being published, promoted, and/or distributed.

*If during the course of your Coaching Call you elect to use our services and want Wahida to put you on the Fast-Track, the fee will then be credited to your brand-new package.

"Turn that Idea or Scene in your Head into a Movie Script or Book" Consulting Program

This program is for you if:

1. You have a scene that plays in your head and you're not sure why or where it comes from. But now you want to know what to do with it. Is it a movie? A book? An episode to a TV pilot? A Broadway Play? A signature speech?

For Your Investment you will receive a 30-minute one-on-one consultation and strategy session with four-time *New York Times* (NYT) Best-seller Wahida Clark. Together you will take that scene or idea in your head and create an outline. Or, if you already know what you want to do with your project, but you need Wahida's assistance in its execution, that can be decided as well. The investment will be credited if you hire her to write a book, outline, script, episode, etc.

"Turn that Idea, Hobby, Expertise, or Training into a Book Now!" Consulting Program

This program is for you if:

1. You have an idea, or you have been collecting data, writing down notes in hopes of getting it all organized into a book. But there's one problem...

You're not quite sure how to organize and structure it.

Great News! You can now gain access to your *One-on-One Gain Clarity and Strategy Session* with a four-time NYT Best Seller and Writing and Publishing Coach. This is your time to share your goals about your idea, hobby, or training with Wahida. During this session, you can explain what you are trying to achieve—your end goal/your vision/and your project details. Your *personalized* Gain Clarity and Strategy Session.

You will use this 40-minute period to gain clarity and outline a strategy that Wahida can put into an itemized Get-It-Done Checklist for you.

After you receive your checklist, you will be able to put your book together, but if you don't want to do it alone, our *"How to Get It Written Program and Publisher's Program"* for nonfiction authors may be an option for you. It includes cover design, professional copyedits by editors who edit for major publishing houses, interior layout, design and book distribution. Your first written book can be the start of Your Own Publishing Empire. And remember, a book is designed to bring in *recurring revenue month after month!*

Nonfiction Program Investment
*email us for details
Memoirs, Biographies, etc., Program Investment
*email us for details
Fiction
*email us for details

"Make Your Book Pop" Consulting Program

This program is for you if:

1. You have a book but are unsure how to launch it . . . **Correctly and Like a Pro!**
2. You want feedback on your cover and overall book presentation
3. You want feedback on your manuscript (from a four-time NYT Best-selling author)
4. You want to establish your books' brand and/or get brand clarity

The "**Make Your Book Pop**" Program includes but is not limited to:

1. Critique and overview
2. Critique of book cover and appearance (Will it stand tall against the other titles on the shelf?)
3. A manuscript read and critique (everyone doesn't request this)
4. Outline Your Blueprint for Your Book Movement to be Launched and Establish Your Brand
5. Newsletter and Facebook Group Consult to Set-up and Launch

*Any critique or feedback can be given verbally or written

"**You Say You Want to Dominate**" **Consulting Program**

This program is for you if:

1. You have a book but are unsure how to launch it . . . **Correctly and Like a Pro!**
2. You want feedback on your cover and overall book presentation
3. You want feedback on your manuscript (from a **four-time NYT Best-selling** author)

4. You want to **Establish** your **Books' Brand** and/or **Get Brand Clarity**
5. You don't have the time to take it to this level on your own and would rather focus on promoting or running your **Book Business**

The **"You Say You Want to Dominate" Consulting Program** includes but is not limited to:

1. Critique and Overview
2. Critique of Book Cover and Appearance (Will it stand tall against the other titles on the shelf?)
3. A Manuscript Read and Critique (everyone doesn't request this)
4. Outline Your Blueprint for Your Book Movement to be Launched and Establish Your Brand
5. Newsletter and Facebook Group Consult to Set-up and Launch
6. New Book, e-book, Hardcover and Audiobook Cover Design
7. Interior Layout files for Paperback, e-book, Hardcover
8. Manuscript Edit
9. Audiobook Narrator
10. Facebook, Instagram, and Twitter Banners
11. Logo Design
12. Book Launch Campaign Set-up (90 Recommended days before Release date)

*Publicist 1 - 3 Months (additional)

"Launch Like a Rock Star or Best-Selling Author" Package

Not everyone thinks they are a Rock or Rap Star. But if you

do, then the "**Launch Like a Rock Star or Best-Selling Author**" **Consulting Package** has your name on it!!! You are undoubtedly in it to win it and want to show your competition NO MERCY!

You get everything that's in the "**You Say You Want to Dominate**" **Package** but is not limited to:

1. Critique and Overview
2. Critique of Book Cover and Appearance (Will it stand tall against the other titles on the shelf?)
3. A Manuscript Read and Critique (everyone doesn't request this)
4. Outline Your Blueprint for Your Book Movement to be Launched and Establish Your Brand
5. Newsletter and Facebook Group Set-up and Launch
6. New Book, e-book, Hardcover and Audiobook Cover Design
7. Interior Layout files for Paperback, e-book, Hardcover
8. Manuscript Edit
9. Audiobook Narrator
10. Facebook, Instagram, and Twitter Banners
11. Logo Design
12. Book Launch Campaign Set-up (90 days before Launch date)
13. Book Publicist for 3 months (included)
14. Video Sales Letter Package
15. Podcast Channel Package
16. YouTube Channel Package
17. Pitch to Television Network Basic Package
18. Book Launch Campaign Set-up and Launch

*Speaking Engagement Publicist 1 - 3 months *optional*

Once again I've given you all of the major tools to write,

publish, and sell. Even if you don't hire our services, this is the blueprint of what and how to publish, launch and continue your quest for growth and knowledge.

Email editor@wclarkdistribution for questions regarding programs. Put in the subject line the name of the program you are interested in.

CONCLUSION

I know that I overdelivered to you my methods of How to turn your Message, Cause, Expertise, and Business Card into a Book. And remember, everyone that is someone has a book. It doesn't have to be 375 pages. It doesn't have to be long and drawn out. In today's swift social media climate, we all want our information uncut, fast delivered on channel WIFM. What's in it for me. Give us want we want, now, no holds barred, no blowing smoke.

I've also given you in this little book the powerful keys of getting your book written/finished and published! I've wiped away all of the excuses!

My mission should you choose to accept, is to make sure that in 45 days or less, you seize this moment. It's finally time to get that draft, outline or book you've been struggling to write into the hands of people who need it. With the weight of accomplishment off your shoulders and another big win is under your belt, you can use your book to spread your message. Now is the time to establish yourself as the expert and get ahead of the competition!

Conclusion

Wahida Clark,
Your #1 Cheerleader

ABOUT THE AUTHOR

Wahida Clark is also known as the Official Queen of Street Literature. She is a Celebrity Book Writing Coach, Celebrity Ghostwriter and author of 22 titles, including 4 New York Times Best-Sellers. She is the Business Development Officer of W. Clark Book Distribution and Executive Producer of the Queen of Street Lit Docuseries and is a lover of anything books ... Writing, Publishing and Promoting.

#1 BEST-SELLER TRAINING

WHY EVERY AUTHOR NEEDS THE STATUS OF BEST-SELLER

WHY DO YOU NEED THIS #1 BEST-SELLER TRAINING WITH CELEBRITY BOOK COACH, WAHIDA CLARK?

- Because you have written a book and you want to Launch it to #1 right out of the gate.
- Because You already published your book but it underperformed and did not make it to the Best-Seller's list, let alone #1!
- Because the stats show that you can become a #1 Best-Seller, even before your book is written and you want to find out for yourself!
- Because you understand that having "#1 Amazon Best-Seller" on your book cover will bring you credibility, authority, influence, speaking engagements, visibility and more!

Thank you for investing in my workbook and #1 Best-Seller Training. Before we get started you need to know the difference in spelling and meaning:
Best-Seller: The Wahida Clark Method
Bestseller: Everyone Else's Method

As always, thank you for supporting me. I know some of you bought the book because you are family, close friends, a fan, or just plain ol' love me!

Please know that I love you more, and I truly appreciate you and thank you for your continuous love and support from the bottom of my heart.

It's amazing how I get phone calls, DMs, tweets, and emails all the time asking how to launch a bestselling book, how to start a publishing company, or how to use a book to become a Superstar/Influencer. I've been asked countless times how one could use a book to establish authority in their field.

I heard you, and I took action. Thank you for trusting and believing that I can lead you to success, whatever your path may be. This book is for those who want to be a #1 Best-Seller—plain and simple. If you have the why, I have the how. And I promise you; it's SHORT and SWEET!

You want the title. You want the #1 Best-Seller belt. You know and understand that having the title "#1 Best-Seller" across your book cover makes all the difference in the universe. It feels amazing to have the title of #1 Bestseller attached to your name and the title of #1 Bestseller in your bio!

For a long time, the question remained: *How do I best serve everyone?* I couldn't figure it out until now! With all the various questions and everyone at a different stage in their writing journey, I realized that each step could be a training all by itself. Therefore, with my schedule being as hectic as it is, I had to figure out how to serve everybody in one setting.

Just Launched 7.16.2021
#1 Best-Seller Training: Finish! Produce! Create! Accelerated Master Class

Publishing is so extensive, and the process starts at "A" and travels letter by letter to "Z." But us spoiled book consumers of the world hold a book in hand and think the process is as quick and simple as the snap of the author's fingers. That's far from the reality! The authors, publishers, and booksellers make it look easy.

The road between "A" and "Z" is long, hard, and convoluted. And the publishing industry is like software; it is constantly changing, upgrading, streamlining, and developing. Then add the everchanging marketing trends and preferences of the readers into the mix, and the evolution never stops. Yet, the foundation of publishing remains the same.

A book always begins as a concept . . . something intangible and barely existing. Then it must be written and, ultimately, finished. But, of course, finishing is only the beginning of production. Producing the book involves editing, formatting, and publishing. Finally, the book has the power of creation, meaning . . . it can create multiple revenue streams all stemming from one source.

The major publishers have their route to get from A to Z. The independent publisher has his route from A to Z. And the indie author has their route. But at Wahida Clark Presents Innovative Publishing, we have our own unique way!

However, the most fun part is this one here: the **#1 Best-Seller Launch**! I love this part of the journey because when the author is ready to launch and become a #1 Best-Seller, that means he or she is in the right mindset. In order to become a #1 Best-Seller, you must BELIEVE in yourself and your book, and being in the zone and achieving that mindset is the only way to get there!

THE MINDSET OF A #1 BEST-SELLER

My audience data shows that the person capable of achieving the #1 **Best-Seller Mindset** can be at any stage in their book journey.

This includes the author whose book is written, but has not been released yet. Another position many authors find themselves in is needing to rerelease their book because they changed the cover, or is rebranding in order to achieve #1 Best-Seller status. Most notably, one might be the author who wants to launch their book to #1 Best-Seller, but the book isn't written it yet!

So, why would you want to launch to #1 even before your book is written? And how can you do that?

Well, here's why.

The fact of the matter is this: once you have the title, no one can take it away from you. You'll be a #1 **Best-Seller for life**, and that can be used to leverage so many new, amazing opportunities.

Before I launched this Master Class, I had to see if it could be done. I needed to be absolutely sure that launching to #1 before the book was written was possible. I've since confirmed it is! And I know that as a new author you can accomplish this feat too! From this experiment I gained new insight and knowledge, and built a training program that will help others achieve the same amount of success I did.

I must make it clear though, that it all comes back to mindset. The Mindset of Execution. How you do it is simple. Begin by setting a date for the future. The catch is you must work hard to get it done because once you upload your book cover, description, price, and commit to a release date etc., you must deliver. You must be disciplined. You must execute. This is not for the excuse makers.

To own the #1 **Best-Seller Mindset**. Ask yourself: Why is it so valuable to be a #1 Best-Seller? How will being a #1 **Best-Seller** change your life?

This demographic (I call them the "executioners") has had a potential growth spurt with their brands, or business, and is at the stage where they either grow or choke. If they commit to growing and have the Best-Seller Mindset, they'll have entered the zone and be on the verge of becoming an influencer. This may be the position you currently find yourself in! Or maybe you already have the Best-Seller Mindset and are on the verge of revamping, relaunching, and rebranding yourself, and you need a #1 Best-Selling title to add to your resumé!

A book can be used to open doors. However, if you think you can you write a book, kick back, put your feet up on the desk, and watch the money stack up in your bank account . . . you are sorely mistaken!

But if you have a book and your goal is to monetize that book, your book can generate many streams of revenue. That's why you want that #1 **Best-Seller** status to increase the potential and quality of the revenue streams. Following my blueprint for a #1 **Best-Seller** launch kicks open the door of monetization. To fully monetize your book and the #1 Best-seller title, you *must* understand that **your book is a business investment.**

Your mission, should you choose to accept it, is to achieve the **#1** *Best-Seller Title and Mindset* in 24 hours or less after launching on the world's largest bookstore (even if you haven't written it yet), positioning yourself to be the influencer or authority in your market.

This triumph will solidify your credibility, help you secure speaking engagements, grant you recognition, and, lastly, allow you to celebrate a huge win!

Now you see why launching to **#1 Best-Seller** is so crucial!

Now Let's Get Started . . .

You must understand that your book is an investment and a business. To begin this journey, you must determine whether your book is fiction or nonfiction. Luckily, this training works very well for both! However, I've noticed that fiction authors must work a little harder than nonfiction authors. This is because the fiction genre has more titles but fewer categories, thus, making the competition much stiffer. Therefore, fiction authors, in my opinion, must ramp up their efforts to make it happen.

It is common practice for authors to target odd, niche categories that their book may or may not have any connection to in an effort to hit #1 Best-Seller. For example, a book about autism may be attached to the computer category. This is a bit exaggerated, but you get my point! Nevertheless, I am not a fan of that "method." And if you use the Wahida Clark method, using categories not connected with your book is entirely unnecessary!

When following my blueprint, the moment you pull the trigger and launch your book, you can become a #1 Best-Seller within 24 hours or less and in your *correct* category.

What you will need:

- #1 Bestseller Core Cheat Sheet
- Book Title
- Book Cover
- Your list of phone numbers, email addresses, and followers on social media that you can DM, tweet, or message about your book.

In regard to your *Book Title*—A Good Name is better than gold.

Yes, your title should stand out, and be catchy!

Even though breaking down my method in this book is a crash course, because we kept it short and simple, it is effective. The first time I followed the blueprint, I only had five-to-six days to launch. And I hit **#1 Best-Seller**. The second time I went through the program just to be sure I had thoroughly learned the system, I only had two days. I had to cram to get everything set up and uploaded within 48 hours. Again, I hit #1 Best-Seller, and this time, in four different categories. So, it works, but you must roll up your sleeves, commit, and give it your all.

You can use this workbook to launch to #1 Best-Seller on your own, or you can hire a coach and invest in a Mastermind Training like I did to launch to #1 Best-Seller with a team or group. Whichever route you need to take, the end goal is the same: *#1 Best-Seller*. Make it happen.

You got this!

I invested in a Master Class to learn how to become a #1 Best-Seller On-Demand! However, this was a costly path. The highest I've seen for any training or Master Class on this subject was $6,500! Yes! But yet, I'm sharing the crash course version for less than what it takes to fill up a tank of gas.

For less than a full tank of gas you are getting ready to learn:

*The Mindset of a #1 Best-Seller
*The Preparation Steps to Hit the #1 Best-Seller Spot (you are going to be surprised)
*Launch Day Strategy/Blueprint
*After Launch Tips to Keep the Momentum Going
*The Why, The How, The What

SETTING UP YOUR KDP ACCOUNT

Why do you want to set up a "Kindle Direct Publishing", or KDP account and sell on Amazon? According to Amazon's Website KDP is **Amazon's self-publishing platform that allows authors to sell their books to Amazon's massive audience**—without the hassle of going through a traditional publishing company. With KDP, authors can create e-books and paperback books, all without any upfront costs or inventory orders."

KDP SIGN-UP

- Go to https: //kdp.amazon.com/en_US/
- Select *Sign-Up* and *Create New Account*.
- Enter your Email Address associated with your desired penname, create a Password, then click *Create Your KDP Account*.
- Amazon will now send a One-Time Verification Password (OTP) to your email or phone. Insert the given code and continue.

- Review and accept the *KDP Agreement* to continue.
- Congratulations! Welcome to your *KDP Dashboard*. You are now almost ready to upload your first title into KDP.

KDP DASHBOARD

The KDP Dashboard is where you go when you need to upload a title, check your sales, launch a marketing campaign, or ask questions inside the KDP Community.

- You should click *My Account* and proceed to enter your Author/Publisher information.
- Enter your banking details for ads, and also so KDP can issue payments.
- Complete the tax survey. This includes Tax Classification, Citizenship, and Identity Information.
- Congratulations! You're now ready to take your first step toward publishing your project with KDP.

KDP UPLOAD PROCESS & MORE

Go to your Bookshelf and click the + symbol to start a project in KDP.

PHASE 1: BOOK DETAILS

Enter title and subtitle of the book, your author name, contributor information, and series data.

Subtitles can be used to augment algorithm search placement with the use of keyword placement.

Ex.

- A Steamy Urban Erotica
- An Epic Fantasy Thriller

ENTER DESCRIPTION

Descriptions should contain keywords and include a hook, brief synopsis, and reasons why readers should buy this book.

KEYWORDS

- This is the most crucial step of the setup process. There are two theories of utility.
- One employs single words or short phrases like "romance," "thriller," or "fantasy."
- The other employs terms like queries used in Amazon searches. For example, "authors like Zane," "books like *Game of Thrones*," or "steamy BWWM romance reads."
- The keywords you select helps Amazon place your book in terms of categories and search, as well as determine what types of customers will potentially see your book within the Amazon platform.
- TIP: Publisher Rocket provides the tools necessary to research which keywords and categories will work best for your title.
- Keywords should be chosen based on sales, number of monthly searches, number of competitors, and level of competition.
- Ensure there are no special characters or commas in keywords and avoid terms like "Best-Seller" or "new."

CATEGORIES

- In the initial setup, only two categories can be selected, and the list provided does not give the user many opportunities for customization.
- Using Publisher Rocket, we can identify the two categories that give us the best opportunity to reach Best-Seller status. From there you can select up to 12

additional keywords (10 plus two alternates) and pick the top two at the time of upload.
- After the title goes live, Amazon can be contacted to add an additional eight categories using the "Contact Us" feature on the website.

PHASE 2: CONTENT

- Before uploading the manuscript triple check for errors.
- Upload the Cover image. Ensure the image meets KDP guidelines to avoid formatting issues.
- Trim size determines how big the actual image needs to be. Canva's paid version works well at resizing images, including PDFs, to the optimal size.
- Make sure that trim size maintains expanded distribution availability.
- Once files are uploaded, use the preview feature to examine the look and feel of the title as it would appear to customers. If there are no issues, proceed to the next steps.

PHASE 3: PRICING AND ROYALTIES

- **KDP Select** means e-book titles will be exclusive to Amazon. This has both pros and cons, and KU (Kindle Unlimited) strategies should be determined prerelease.
- List the title at the prearranged price. Ensure pricing is consistent in US, AU, UK, and CA marketplaces.

LENDING

- If a title is **KDP Select**, this is automatically selected.
- Lending allows people who purchased the book to lend it for a limited time, like a library book. When a title is not in KU (**KDP Select on the readers' end**), I suggest selecting Lending.

SUBMIT TITLE

Congratulations! Your title is being processed by KDP for availability in the marketplace!

POST-SUBMISSION CONSIDERATIONS

There are times when KDP will reject your project due to errors or formatting issues. These are addressed in two ways:

- Via Email. KDP will issue an email detailing why your project was rejected.
- Quality Notification on your Bookshelf in your Dashboard. This will be a red outlined box with a yellow caution symbol.

QUALITY NOTIFICATIONS

The KDP Quality Notification system allows you to fix issues Amazon, or customers, have identified as a quality issue. From the Quality Notifications Dashboard, you can

- Review issues
- Make corrections
- Upload revised files, and

- Track the status of revisions

COMMON ISSUES

Cover/Trim Sizes

- Use software like Canva Pro to resize the image to proper specifications.
- Using the KDP Cover Template or KDP Cover Calculator will help avoid this problem.

MANUSCRIPT FORMATTING

- Sometimes, KDP rejects a project due to manuscript formatting problems.
- If you run into this issue, it's worth downloading programs like Kindle Create to reformat your work. This program uses a special Kindle Format designed to seamlessly integrate into KDP.

SPELLING AND GRAMMAR ISSUES

- Customers, or Amazon, can and will flag a title for spelling and grammar. A read-through and editorial services can best remedy these types of issues.

MORE SECRET SAUCE AND STRATEGIES KDP, CATEGORIES, ETC...

Be sure to watch and study the short video (below) on the KDP page.

After you set up your KDP account, go back and familiarize yourself with the platform. Click around. Go in, play with the tabs, and familiarize yourself with the drop-down menus for Bookshelf & Reports.

The Bookshelf Tab is where your book title's metadata is. You can find your book by its cover or by its title.

The Reports Tab drop-down menu is where all your sales data is kept.

So, don't be intimidated. You can't mess up anything! Get very comfortable and familiar with those drop-down menus.

This is where you track your money and see how many books you have sold in real time.

YOUR E-BOOK COVER

Do judge a book by its cover! Always keep that in mind. You can use the Amazon platform to generate a free eBook cover, or you can outsource to places like Fiverr, 99 designs, or WCP's preferred partner, Designs by Nuance. As an author and a publisher, I have used them all. As an author, my first choice is our preferred partner, Designs by Nuance, followed by 99 designs. I really like both of these options for nonfiction.

YOUR BOOK DESCRIPTION

Your book description, also known as the back-cover synopsis, can range from 40–80 or more words. To me, less is better, but the bottom line is the book description is there to sell the book. So, even if your book description isn't already written, go grab a book off the shelf, turn it over, and read the description, or go to Amazon and read the descriptions in your genre to stimulate your creativity, even if you haven't written one yet.

YOUR COPYRIGHT PAGE

Even though the copyright page is optional in e-books, I always include it. It helps your e-book look more professional, and you need it anyway for your paperback and hardback copies.

Here is a sample of a fiction copyright page:

This is a work of fiction. Names, characters, places, and incidents either are the product of the author's imagination or are used fictitiously. Any resemblance to actual persons, living or dead, business establishments, events, or locales is entirely coincidental.

Wahida Clark Presents Publishing
60 Evergreen Place
Suite 904A
East Orange, New Jersey 07018
1(866)-910-6920 www.wclarkpublishing.com
www.wclarkdistribution.com

Copyright 2019 © by Aisha Hall
All rights reserved. This book, or parts thereof, may not be reproduced in any form without permission.
Library of Congress Cataloging-In-Publication Data:
Aisha Hall
Baltimore Raw
ISBN 13-digit 9781944992590 (paper)
ISBN 13-digit 9781944992651 (ebook)
ISBN 13-digit 9781944992637 (Hardcover)

LCCN: 201000000
1. Sex - 2. Lies - 3. Infidelity - 4. African American - HIV - 5. Homosexuality - 6. Violence - 7. Relationships
Cover design and layout by Nuance Art, LLC
Book design by NuanceArt@wclarkpublishing.com
Edited by Linda Wilson
Proofreader Rosalind Hamilton

PRE-ORDER OR NOT TO PRE-ORDER

Pre-order lets you offer customers the option to pre-order your book as much as one year before the release date. Why would you want to set the date as far out as possible? So that you can polish up your manuscript and your brand. You want to tighten up your launch campaign as well as promote your Launch Day! This is also the opportunity to create any course content related to your book, such as trainings and live events. On your book's release date, customers who preordered your book will automatically have it delivered to their Kindle.

If your book is ready, meaning everything on the following Cheat Sheet is checked off, and you are prepared to release ASAP, then check the "I am ready to release my book now" button. You are telling Amazon that you are ready now and that you understand that your book will be "Live" and on sale within 42–72 hours, and in exchange, readers can now buy multiple orders and share the link with their friends to help you get more book sales.

Once you determine, pre-order or no pre-order, (if you elect to allow pre-orders choose your release date), hit save and continue.

KEYWORDS

Keywords are critical. However, you should not use words that are in the title of your book! You should get good at being able to choose the right ones. If you don't use keyword research software such as Publisher Rocket, use the KDP help page to search for keywords. *Make it your business to visit KDP and search to study the following subjects:

- **How to add and update keywords**

- Best practices
- Useful keyword types
- Keywords to avoid
- Categories
- Choosing categories
- Add or update categories

DRM (DIGITAL RIGHTS MANAGEMENT)

Enable DRM Yes—you want to check *Yes.*

If you're publishing an eBook, you'll decide if you want to enable Digital Rights Management (DRM). DRM is intended to inhibit unauthorized access to or copying of digital content files. Some authors desire the protection that DRM offers; others want readers to share their work to reach a wider audience and thus, choose not to enable DRM.

TIP: DRM is a one-time option. It can't be changed after you publish. *****Most Important Part of the #1 Best-Seller Training**

PRE-LAUNCH DAY PREP

In junior high school, I was a cheerleader. The cheerleader is there to encourage the team. Be that support! Have their back! Clap for the team when they are winning. Cheer for the team when they are losing. When I send emails to my mailing list, I often sign *"from Wahida Clark, your #1 Cheerleader."*

To have a successful launch, you will need to be a cheerleader and form a squad! Your squad is your dedicated actions takers. Your squad is ride or die. Your squad will fight for you, and your squad will say yes to giving you support whenever you may need it.

Your squad needs to know computers, be willing to help with promo, utilize social media, and call family and friends to get everyone to buy your book on launch day! So be particular when picking your squad.

THE CHEERLEADER/TEAM CAPTAIN

As the Team Captain of the cheerleading squad, you must stay focused and positive for yourself and the squad. You will have to duck and dodge the negativity and keep the squad positive. Expect people to support you, help you, and get excited for you but also be prepared for the haters, those who hate to see you having some success. Despite all the haters, you will have to stay focused on your squad because they need your full, undivided attention and energy.

You want to be well rested on launch day and focused on your energy because it will be shared and spread around. A #1 Best-Seller Book launch is an all-day event. So, if your launch kickoff is at 10:00 a.m., you shouldn't finish until midnight.

THINGS YOU NEED TO PROVIDE FOR YOUR SQUAD:

Set up a Facebook Group aka your Book Launch Squad, where the Squad can invite others and where you can post and keep everybody up to date.

A Phone Script that is tailored to your audience for your squad to use when they call their friends and family to ask them to support your new book.

Go to FB Community Live and the other social media platforms and go Live telling everyone who you are, why you wrote the book, and who you are helping.

Social media posts talking about the Book Campaign. At launch, your book should be discounted ($.99–$2.99) for 24 hours only! Your posts should tell everyone to share the link and confirm that they ordered it because you need help getting the word out.

An email script describing your book, including the links, would be helpful. The point of the email is to tell everyone to grab a copy of your book and let them know what your book's message is.

Make it about the reader and your book's message, not about you as the author. Let them know that the more people buy your book, the more people you can help.

HOW TO GROW YOUR BOOK LAUNCH SQUAD FROM 0–60 FOLLOWERS

Go Live telling everyone who you are, why you wrote the book, and who you desire to help according to your book subject. Invite everyone in the audience to hop on the train and to help you on your journey. It is also a great idea to call your friends and family to get them to **commit** to helping you as well. Lock them in!

That's how you go from 0-60 building your Book Launch Squad.

*To do on Launch Day to Track your Sales and Success

Keep an eye on the Bookshelf **Reports** and **Sales** Tab to track your book sales.

Keep an eye on the **Product Details Page.** The Product Details Page tracks your sales ranking. Just as this author has the #1 spot, this is what we want as well. The rankings are updated hourly.

Product details
ASIN : B0773RQ55P
Publisher : Joseph Murphy (July 23, 2021)
Publication date : July 23, 2021
Language : English
File size : 467 KB
Text-to-Speech : Enabled
Screen Reader : Supported
Enhanced typesetting : Enabled
X-Ray : Enabled
Word Wise : Enabled
Print length : 224 pages
Lending : Not Enabled
Best Sellers Rank: #7,534 in Kindle Store (See Top 100 in Kindle Store)
#1 in Money & Monetary Policy (Kindle Store)
#1 in Dreams (Kindle Store)
#4 in Personal Money Management (Kindle Store)
Customer Reviews: ★★★★☆ ~ 36,050 ratings

*Best-Seller Trait: Your goal should be to remain in the Top 100.

HOW MANY BOOKS DO YOU HAVE TO SELL TO HIT #1 BEST-SELLER?

Only the KDP Algorithm can answer that. But every sale counts, so that's why you have to follow the training and on Launch Day where grind hard and really drive those your team and those sales. *That* is the secret ingredient. **Aim** to sell a minimum of 100 books during your spurt.

Post-Launch Tips

Postlaunch is when the campaign is down to the last two hours and after midnight when the campaign is over.

Have your squad reach out to readers to urge them to share confirmation that they purchased the book. Then you can thank your readers personally for buying your book!

Check your KDP Dashboard hourly and share with your squad as your book rises higher and higher in the ranking. Keep your squad fired up and congratulate them and honor them for helping you launch your book to #1 Best-Seller.

It is important to note that there is a "Top 100 Paid" and a "Top 100 Free" list. There is also a "New Releases" list. You want to be #1 in general. For the life of your book, your goal should be to keep it on the "Top 100 Paid" list. The "Top 100 Free" list should be your goal *if* you only use the book as a promo item or lead magnet.

After your book hits #1, generate a #1 Best-Seller Sticker and use it for marketing and promo on your book cover and social media.

Remember to thank everyone who purchased your book. This will make it more likely that they will post a review if you ask them to do so! You can also ask them to post about your book in your Facebook Group.

A press release is another great tool! Having a press release written for your achievement of #1 **Best-Seller** status will only keep the momentum going. I would have this written even before the launch.

www.ingramcontent.com/pod-product-compliance
Lightning Source LLC
LaVergne TN
LVHW020135080526
838202LV00047B/3945